MINNESOTA LOONS

Joyce Mrosla

NORTH STAR PRESS OF ST. CLOUD, INC.
Saint Cloud, Minnesota

This book is gratefully dedicated to Jim.
Without him, these photographs would not have been possible.

This is a photo journey of loons on Rassier Lake and Little Watab Lake in St. Joseph, Minnesota.
A gracious couple on Little Watab built the loon nest platform from birch logs. We are very thankful for that effort.

The loon eggs hatched on May 28th. The last time we saw the loons on the lake was August 22nd.

ISBN: 978-0-87839-445-6

Printed in the United States of America by Sentinel Printing, St. Cloud, Minnesota.

Published by
North Star Press of St. Cloud, Inc.
PO Box 451
St. Cloud MN 56302
www.northstarpress.com

The common loon became the Minnesota state bird in 1961.
Minnesota has more common loons than any other state, except Alaska.

Loons have a wingspan of up to five feet. They have dense bones to help them in diving.

Loons prefer lakes of twenty-five or more acres. They like water that has both shallow areas and deep depths for shelter and diving.

The loon has four basic calls: the tremolo, the wail, the hoot, and the yodel.

Loons will rub their heads on their backs to waterproof their head feathers.

Loon eggs hatch in twenty-six to thirty-one days. Males and females take turns incubating the eggs.

Loons rise up on the water and flap their wings
to stretch and preen their feathers.
They must take excellent care of their feathers
to maintain their water repelling qualities.

6

A loon vigilantly protects its eggs. Many creatures, including eagles, racoons, foxes, and even family pets, can attack loons. These turtles are sunning themselves on the nest edges and do not pose much threat.

This chick is newly hatched.

This baby is climbing aboard for a ride. It is one day old.

10

These babies are safely tucked under the parent's wing one day after hatching.

It looks like this day-old loon has a lot of questions about its new world.

This one-day-old chick waits for its lunch.

Within twenty-four hours, the loons have moved to a nursery away from the nest for safety.

The chicks are now three days old.

The chicks are now nine days old. Male and female loons look alike, although males are usually larger.

Very young chicks can make short dives and catch small fish.

Nine days old and buoyantly swimming along.

At sixteen days old, these chicks are getting too big to ride on their parents' backs, but they stay close by their parents' sides.   21

These young loons are nineteen days old.

The loon is a splendid diver and has great vision underwater. Loons can dive more than 100 feet.

These little ones always seem to be hungry.

They are thirty-three days old.

It's feeding time again.

This chick is six weeks old.
Parents feed them for the first several weeks.

A loon's legs are set far back on its body. This is ideal for diving but not well suited for walking on land.

The origin of the word loon means "lame" or "clumsy." It probably got its name for the awkward way it walks on land.

Loons belong to the order Gaviiformes, of which there are five modern species.

A tremolo call is made when a loon is excited or agitated. It is the only call used in flight.

A yodel is a territorial call given only by males

A wail call is used to locate other loons in the area.

A hoot call is used by parents to keep siblings together.

One of the loons' unique features are their vibrant red eyes.

The young loons are now seven weeks old. The second coat of downy feathers have appeared.
They will moult one more time before they can fly.

A loon's primary weapon is its bill.

The baby loons are seven weeks old.
The average life expectancy of a loon is between fifteen and thirty years.

Loons show great acrobatic talents while stretching or preening their feathers.
Their waterproof feathers prevent the water from reaching their skin.

A loon can stay underwater for more than five minutes.

These parents continue to feed their young at about seven weeks of age.
A loon's diet consists primarily of fish.

This loon is about eight weeks old.
It is becoming more independent.

A young loon is taking a nap. It is about eight weeks old.

A loon may spend five to ten minutes trying to orient its prey so it can be swallowed head first.

The young loons are about eight weeks old in these photos.

At about nine weeks old, this loon is starting to look sleek.

This young loon seems to be admiring its reflection.

At around eleven or twelve weeks, loons are able to gather almost all of their own food. This loon is ten weeks old.

This loon is now twelve weeks. Loons learn to fly around eleven to twelve weeks old.

A loon needs a long stretch of open water to act as a runway for takeoff.

They can fly more than seventy-five miles per hour.

This last photo was taken August 22nd, just a little over twelve weeks after hatching. Most loons from Minnesota migrate to the Gulf of Mexico coast for the winter months.